FREEDOM THROUGH Forgiving

A Workbook for Everyone Who Has Been Hurt by Someone

Dwight Lee Wolter

CompCare® Publishers
Minneapolis, Minnesota

Cataloging-in-Publication Data

Wolter, Dwight Lee.
    Freedom through forgiving: a workbook for everyone who has been
hurt by someone/Dwight Lee Wolter.
    p. cm.
    ISBN: 0-89638-238-4
    1. Forgiveness. I. Title.
    BF637.F67W65 1993   158.2
                                                     QB192-20397

Cover design by Maclean and Tuminelly

Inquiries, orders, and catalog requests should be addressed to
CompCare Publishers
3850 Annapolis Lane
Minneapolis, Minnesota 55447
Call toll free 800/328-3330
or 612/559-4800

6   5   4   3   2   1
98   97   96   95   94   93

This book is dedicated to
Jane Thomas Noland,
my friend, Celeste's friend,
who, in 1989, acquired my first book,
which led to my dream of becoming a published author.

I will confide in you, gentle reader,
that Jane is my editor and is therefore,
by definition,
much in need of forgiveness.

I have learned to trust and respect Jane immensely,
as she has edited four of my books.
And I am willing to bet that,
by the time you read this,
she will have edited
this dedication page as well.

Blessings and health to you, Jane,
upon your retirement from publishing.
And now that you have turned sixty-five,
I wish you blessings and health
on the second half of your life.

CONTENTS

Introduction

What Is Unforgivable?   1

What Is Forgiveness?   19

Expectations   31

Before We Can Forgive   41

Obstacles to Forgiveness   47

Face to Face with Anger   63

Blaming Ourselves, Blaming Others   77

Anger, Blame, and Forgiveness   85

Forgiving Others   91

Forgiving Ourselves   101

Forgiveness: Tools and Mistakes   113

Going Home   121

Being on Your Own Side   125

Dear Me. . .   131

INTRODUCTION

Threadbook is the long-awaited companion to Dwight Lee Wolter's best-selling book, *Forgiving Our Parents*. A lot has happened to Wolter in the years following the publication of *Forgiving Our Parents*. He has presented workshops throughout the country and has fine-tuned the many tools of exploring the choice and process of forgiveness. He now offers these tools in this workbook.

Wolter says, "People have asked me why I waited three years from the time *Forgiving Our Parents* was released to write the *Freedom through Forgiving* workbook. The answer is simple. I wanted to wait until I was sure of the response to the process offered here. Through the workshops I have conducted, I now know that this workbook will walk people through the specific steps of forgiveness, utilizing the tools available along the way."

Events in his own life since the publication of *Forgiving Our Parents* have taught Wolter even more about forgiveness. His mother died the day the book was published. As Wolter says, "Holding on to blame and anger, while waiting for my mother to assume responsibility for her part in our troubled relationship, backfired the day she died. Reconciliation with her became impossible, but forgiveness did not. People we are struggling to forgive need not even be living. A lot of healing has taken place in my relationship with my mother since her death. I wish it could have happened while she was still alive. This workbook will help others to become more willing and able to consider the choice and process of forgiveness of any significant persons in their lives—spouses, bosses, friends, siblings—and possibly to avoid the abrupt end to communication that I experienced with my mother."

This workbook reiterates the basic tenets of forgiveness that were offered in *Forgiving Our Parents*. It also guides readers on a hypothetical return trip home—or to other settings where abuse and neglect may have occurred—while providing strategies for self-protection and some reasons for guarded optimism. It helps readers discover and assess the realistic and unrealistic expectations they hold for themselves and others. Through specific exercises, this book will give you an opportunity. . .

- to decide whether to confront the abusers;

- to assess motives, secret agendas, and tainted perceptions;

- to reword societal and doctrinal statements about forgiveness into more palatable and usable forms (for example, "To err is human, to forgive divine" can be changed to read "To err is human, to forgive is optional");

- to write a letter to the people you feel have wronged you and to write a response from them;

- to discover the relationship between forgiving yourself and forgiving others;

- to write a love letter to yourself.

Guided visualization and meditation exercises will help you. . .

- heal in places where words can't go;

- learn the futility of withholding love as a response to not having been loved;

- learn to separate people from their behaviors;

- take power back from others and place it within yourself, where it belongs.

You will notice that usually a brief introduction precedes each exercise. Then, after you finish the exercise, a conclusion follows on the same topic. I strongly suggest that you do not skip over the exercise or read the conclusion before doing the work. In these conclusions, I may be able to provide you with some insights into forgiveness. I also may be able to show you some of the issues I am working on at the present time. But I can never do the work for you. No one can fall in love for you. No one can die for you. And no one can forgive for you. This is your own noble process.

WHAT IS UNFORGIVABLE?

IT'S SIMPLY UNFORGIVABLE!

Has someone done something that you consider unforgivable?

Do you find yourself unable to "let go" of that person and move on from that episode or time in your life?

Do you think your difficulty in forgiving has caused you more distress than you deserve or are willing to tolerate?

Does what you consider to be unforgivable reach beyond people you know or what has happened to you personally? Are there certain acts or individuals in history that you simply cannot or will not forgive?

What do you consider to be unforgivable?

- ❑ Sex discrimination.
- ❑ Child abuse.
- ☒ Drunk driving.
- ☒ Genocide.
- ❑ Spouse-stealing?
- ❑ Drug-peddling?
- ❑ Smoking in a crowded room?
- ❑ Firing someone for reasons of personal power?
- ❑ Other:

Acting in such away to cause others to suffer the consequences instead of the consequences be personal

Who, in your eyes, is unforgivable?

❑ Your boss.

❑ The president of your company.

❑ The president of your country.

☒ Hitler.

❑ Hitler's mother.

❑ Your mother.

❑ The man who shot the Pope.

❑ Pontius Pilate.

☒ Other:

Howard _____

_____

On the following pages, jot down a few unforgivable persons, actions, behaviors, attitudes—whatever pops into your mind. Don't think too much! Don't worry about complete sentences. Your list doesn't have to reflect events that happened to you directly.

My List of Unforgivables

PEOPLE

Are there any people in the world or in your past or present life whom you consider unforgivable?

_____

_____

_____

_____

_____

_____

_____

_____

_____

What ages are these people? (Is it easier to forgive a child than a grown-up?)

_____

_____

_____

_____

_____

_____

ACTIONS

What actions, either in history or in your personal life, do you consider to be unforgivable?

_____

_____

_____

_____

_____

_____

_____

_____

_____

Are there any places you cannot or will not visit because you can't forget what took place there?

_____

_____

_____

_____

_____

_____

BEHAVIORS

What behaviors of others—behaviors that have caused you harm—
do you consider to be unforgivable?

_____

_____

_____

_____

_____

What are some unforgivable things that people might do to their
bodies or allow to happen to their bodies?

_____

_____

_____

_____

ATTITUDES

Do some people have attitudes toward themselves or others that
you consider to be unforgivable? What are they?

_____

_____

_____

_____

_____

Now that you have made a brief list of your "unforgivables," take a moment to select the one from your list that you consider the "most unforgivable."

Answer the questions on the following page, including *why* you consider the item you selected to be unforgivable.

Write about the feelings that are coming up as you think about what is unforgivable.

Go into it. Dig deeper. Express what you believe. Don't judge yourself. No one is looking. Tell your truth. Believe in what you are writing.

Begin now.

The Single Most Unforgivable Thing I Know of Today

What do I consider the MOST unforgivable?

_____

_____

_____

_____

Why do I consider this to be unforgivable?

- ❑ Religious reasons.
- ❑ Moral or ethical reasons.
- ❑ It happened to me.
- ❑ It's illegal.
- ❑ Everyone in my family agrees that it's unforgivable.
- ❑ The person responsible knew better.
- ❑ Other:

_____

_____

_____

Use the above questions to write a few words in the following space about your answer above.

_____

_____

_____

_____

_____

_____

List the feelings that came up as you thought and wrote about this topic.

_____

_____

_____

_____

_____

_____

_____

_____

_____

_____

_____

_____

_____

_____

_____

Good work!

Take a moment to read what you have written. Now, try an experiment: If possible, try to read your answers as if you have never met the person who wrote them. In other words, try to step back a little emotionally and read your answers as if you have just discovered them in a book written by an author you have never met.

Do you agree with what was written about what is unforgivable?

_____

What do you think the person felt while writing it?

_____

_____

_____

_____

What do you feel for or about the person who wrote it?

- ❏ Compassion.
- ❏ Sympathy.
- ❏ Sadness.
- ❏ Disgust.
- ❏ Anger.
- ❏ Love.
- ❏ Other:

_____

_____

Do you think everyone in the world would agree that what was written about is unforgivable?

_____

_____

_____

Is there anyone in the world who might disagree?

_____

_____

_____

How could that person who disagrees possibly forgive something unforgivable? Is that person. . .

❑ evil?

❑ mentally ill?

❑ naive?

❑ foolish?

❑ saintly?

❑ a perpetual victim?

❑ other?

_____

_____

Now we are about to embark on a very difficult task.

In the following section, answer the questions from the perspective of someone who can forgive the unforgivable.

If you want the forgiving person to appear unrealistic or passive, or even stupid—then get into it!

If the forgiving person begins to seem like your parent or someone else you know, let that happen too.

Though it may be difficult, try to let the forgiver have a say.

A Few Words from a Person Who Can Forgive the Unforgivable

Please answer the following questions:

I feel that I should forgive because the person. . .
     (Example: . . . didn't intend to do it.)

_____

_____

_____

_____

Basically, I think that people are. . .
     (Examples: . . . good, ignorant, "only human.")

_____

_____

_____

_____

I believe that people who forgive are. . .
(Examples: . . . more generous, more spiritual than those who are unforgiving.)

Here is what I get out of it if I forgive others. . .
(Example: . . . peace of mind)

Use the above examples as a springboard to get your thoughts moving. Think of as many of your own examples as possible.

In Summary: A Few Thoughts about Forgiving the Unforgivable

Now, please answer these questions:

What did you learn from your investigation into what is unforgivable?

_____

_____

_____

_____

Are you as convinced now about what is unforgivable as you were before you began the exercise?

_____

_____

_____

_____

Did you gain any insights into why someone might wish to consider forgiving the unforgivable?

_____

_____

_____

_____

Did you gain any insights into yourself from your reaction to the hypothetical person who is willing to forgive the unforgivable?

_____

_____

_____

_____

Are you being judgmental of that person?

_____

_____

_____

_____

Are you being judgmental of yourself?

_____

_____

_____

Is it okay for you to judge others?

_____

_____

_____

Why?

_____

_____

_____

_____

_____

Why not?

_____

_____

_____

_____

_____

Do you find that you judge yourself harshly for harshly judging others?

_____

_____

_____

_____

_____

_____

_____

A STORY ABOUT FORGIVENESS

Several years ago a very prominent religious leader was riding in an open car in a motorcade when he was shot and wounded by a would-be assassin. When the religious leader was sufficiently healed, he went to the prison that housed the gunman. From my understanding of what happened, the religious leader chatted with the man, had lunch with him, prayed with him, and forgave him.

My first reaction was that the religious leader must be crazy. Why would you want to forgive a person who blew a hole in you?

Then it dawned on me! He must have forgiven him because that is what religious leaders are supposed to do! They're the ones who are always talking about peace, forgiveness, and turning the other cheek.

Then I had another thought. What if the religious leader forgave his assailant for all the obvious reasons, and, in addition to that, maybe the religious leader wanted to heal himself.

Perhaps the religious leader was tired of walking around angry at the man who shot him. Maybe he realized that, while he was focusing so much of his time, energy, and attention on the man and his motives, the gunman could, at that very moment, simply be watching television, eating lunch, and relaxing. Maybe the religious leader was tired of giving some nut with a gun the power to upset him. Maybe he was tired of living in fear of the day when the assailant would be released from prison.

Seen in this light, forgiving someone is not only religiously and socially appropriate, desirable, or mandated, it also may be gloriously selfish.

Forgiving can be an act of healing
our relationships with others.

Forgiving can be an act of healing
our relationships with ourselves.

WHAT IS FORGIVENESS?

WHAT IS FORGIVENESS, ANYWAY?

forgive **1. to excuse for a fault or offense; pardon 2. to renounce anger or resentment against 3. to absolve from payment of. Synonyms: excuse, condone.**

—American Heritage Dictionary
Second College Edition

Forgiveness is a natural function of a healthy organism. Children want to forgive their parents. Lovers strive to forgive each other. Trees bend to forgive the wind.

Forgiveness is a choice. Although forgiveness is often discussed as if it were a mandate, it is always a choice. Some people are too eager to forgive because they want to leapfrog over the pain of realizing and accepting what happened to them. Some people pretend to be able to forgive because they are embarrassed that they don't know how. Some people pretend to forgive so they will look better to others. Some people are anxious to forgive. Some people have pledged never to forgive. But no one truly forgives without wanting to forgive.

Forgiveness is a process. It is not a single, momentous act. Forgiveness is like hunger. If you get hungry and eat a sandwich, your hunger will go away. But I guarantee you it will return again. Eating once does not mean you have "done" hunger. And forgiving once does not mean you have "done" forgiveness.

The nature of those we are striving to forgive is that they may do something again that will cause us to consider the choice of forgiving them again.

Since forgiveness is a process, at any point in time we have the choice of abandoning the pursuit. We can choose to stay in anger and blame, if that is what we feel we need. We can choose to leave a relationship rather than to forgive the other.

Forgiveness requires time and timing. We can choose to be patient with the process. We can choose when and where to offer forgiveness, so as to increase the possibility of its being accepted. The only time limits are those we impose upon ourselves.

Forgiveness is never a formula. Despite what others might tell us, there is no socially sanctioned, morally mandated, psychologically correct, spiritually perfect approach to forgiveness.

Forgiveness is a mystery. We live in a culture that preaches great gobs of forgiveness yet practices very little of it. We live in a holding-onto-resentment culture rather than in a forgiving one. Where is the evidence of forgiveness—or tolerance—in the my-way-is-right practices of some of our religious crusaders?

Few of us believe that we can directly effect world peace through our personal efforts. But we can. We can begin global change by changing ourselves. We can tap our vast reservoir of personal power. We can learn the art of forgiveness in our dealings with ourselves and our relationships. And we can carry what we learn into our world.

Forgiveness is about us, not about "them." When we realize the rewards of forgiving, it doesn't matter so much whether our attempts at forgiveness are well received by others or not.

Before we choose to forgive, we must ask ourselves two very important questions. Please write your answer in the space provided below each question. The simple act of writing imprints on the mind and soul in deep and mysterious ways.

1. Am I willing to consider the choice and process of forgiveness?

_____

2. Am I willing to do what it takes?

_____

If your answer to these questions is yes, then let's continue.

No matter what our specific situation is, it is very important to remember that forgiveness is about us more than it is about *them*. More specifically, it is about our *perceptions* of us and them.

Healing through Forgiveness

We think, act, and feel,

not on reality,

but on our perceptions

of reality.

What we hope to heal

are our perceptions

of our parents, loved ones,

and others.

We don't heal people.

We don't heal relationships.

We heal our perceptions

of our relationships.

WE CHOOSE OUR PERCEPTIONS

Allow me to tell you a story.

Twin sisters are deciding whether to go home to celebrate their mother's fiftieth birthday.

Relationships in their family have been difficult. Their father is an alcoholic. He seldom speaks to his wife or daughters. He works hard, comes home, eats dinner, and watches television until it is time to go to bed.

The mother, however, talks all the time. She has a hard time staying out of other people's business. Some would call her a nag. She is never cruel or violent, but she is very opinionated. She is convinced that the world would be a better place if only everyone would take her advice.

One daughter decides to go home for her mother's birthday celebration.

The other daughter decides not to go home.

To answer the questions on pages 24-26, use your imagination and step into the shoes of the daughter who decided not to go home.

For questions on pages 26-28, use your imagination and step into the shoes of the daughter who decided to go home. Explain why you are willing to go home, despite the troubles you will most likely find there.

Try not to think too much as you are writing. Shoot from the hip. Remember that you are writing not about you, but about the twin sisters.

Take a moment to envision the sisters before you begin.

Begin now.

Why I Decided Not to Go Home to Celebrate My Mother's Birthday

Please answer these questions:

This is what I think of my mother at the moment:

_____

_____

_____

This is what I think of my family's reaction to my absence:

_____

_____

_____

This is what I think of myself for deciding to stay away:

_____

_____

_____

Yes, it is my mother's birthday and I know I will feel some hurt, but that feeling is outweighed by the following considerations (choose one or more and/or add your own):

- ❏ I can't tolerate the same old scenes.
- ❏ I want to sever all family ties—they mean nothing to me.
- ❏ I want to punish her for being unhelpful and obnoxious.
- ❏ If I go, she'll just interfere more.
- ❏ I can't put up with my dad's alcoholic behavior and the way my mom lets him walk all over her.

_____

_____

_____

My deepest, most secret, most private reason for not going is:

_____

_____

_____

_____

_____

This is what I hope my mother will feel when I'm not there:

_____

_____

_____

_____

_____

This is what I fear the most as a result of my not going:

_____

_____

_____

_____

_____

Why I Decided to Go Home to Celebrate My Mother's Birthday

Now that we have looked at reasons why someone might choose *not* to go home, let's look at reasons *for* choosing to go home.

Choose from among the following, or add your own:

❑ Her age and health are failing.

❑ I'm attempting to mend fences.

❑ I'm trying one more time to see if she can live up to what I expect a mother to be.

❑ It's expected of me.

❑ Other reasons (write as much or as little as you like):

_____

_____

_____

_____

_____

_____

This is what my family would think of me if I stayed away:

_____

_____

_____

This is what I would think of me if I stayed away:

_____

_____

_____

_____

This is what my mother would think of me if I stayed away:

_____

_____

_____

It's true that my mother hurt me and still sometimes drives me crazy, but:

_____

_____

_____

_____

These are the ways in which I will benefit if I go to the birthday party:

_____

_____

_____

_____

_____

_____

Which Sister Was Right?

Go back and read the pages you wrote for the two sisters.

Which sister was right in her decision? (This is not a silly question, and yours will not be a silly answer. Be as brief as you like.)

_____

_____

_____

_____

_____

_____

_____

_____

_____

The Dilemma of the Two Sisters: Some Conclusions

Neither sister was right, and neither sister was wrong. Their choices were based on feelings. And there are no such things as right or wrong feelings.

There are certainly feelings that make you comfortable and feelings that make you uncomfortable. But there are no right or wrong feelings. Feelings are just feelings. Feelings just are.

When we stop judging our feelings and condemning ourselves for having the "wrong" ones, we inch closer to the place where true forgiveness can happen.

Perhaps one twin decided not to go home because she feels smothered by the mother. She feels like a victim of "smotherlove." She feels that her mother is a controlling nag who sticks her nose into everyone else's affairs. And all the while the mother is meddling—and ignoring or denying her own problems—she is married to a drunk. This daughter feels too angry to go home. This daughter refuses to go home and dutifully play her role in the family soap opera. She also secretly hopes that her absence will hurt the mother.

The other daughter can't wait to go home. She is extremely excited about the mother's birthday and has bought her an expensive gift. This daughter also realizes that the mother is a nag, but she is more accepting of her. She knows that she didn't get enough love from either her mother or her father. But at least she realizes her mother loved her. Her father might as well have been dead. He numbly and silently sat in front of the television during her entire childhood. The mother confused worrying with love, and tried to compensate for the emotionally absent father. She failed. But at least she tried. At least she cared.

Both daughters are right. Both daughters are wrong. Neither daughter is right. Neither daughter is wrong.

Forgiveness is not a moral issue. Forgiveness is a choice. We choose the way we perceive others and our relationship to them. Forgiveness is a shift from one perception to another. We are free to heal the ways in which we choose to perceive people.

Our work on forgiveness makes a shift in perception possible.

EXPECTATIONS

EXPECTATIONS

A lot of forgiveness work involves expectations of what will happen to us when we forgive—as well as to those we are trying to forgive. Many of us have been told that we expect too much. Others of us believe that we don't deserve to expect anything. Several of us have given up having expectations because we are so used to being disappointed.

No matter how we feel about expectations, they remain a huge part of our work on forgiveness. If we could simply adjust our expectations of how we and others are "supposed to" behave, we would save ourselves a lot of grief. If we could be more *realistic* about who people are and what they are capable of, we would have done much of our forgiveness work before we even began this difficult process. For example, when I allowed my father to be himself, he no longer felt that I was pointing an accusing finger at him, and he was able to feel more comfortable with me. He began to open up and confide in me some of the issues as he saw them.

Take a few moments now to write (on page 34) a brief list of your expectations for yourself and the people you are trying to forgive. You need not try to be rational or fair. Let your true expectations surface. Jot down the first thoughts that leap into your mind. Then pause a moment and let deeper expectations surface.

If you believe that forgiveness can't really change anything—if you have no expectations—write about why you think you don't and what that feels like.

If you feel you don't deserve to have expectations, write about the expectations you would have if you deserved to have them.

The following page is divided in half. On the left side, write about the expectations you have for yourself as a result of your work on forgiveness. Write about what you hope to gain (or lose), what you hope to accomplish, changes you expect to see in your own feelings, beliefs, and attitudes. Write about what you expect to feel like once you have gained insight about forgiveness and have been able to forgive.

On the right side, write about what expectations you have for the person or persons you are trying to forgive. What will it be like for others after you have done your work on forgiveness?

The worksheet begins with a hypothetical example in each column.

Start your lists now.

What I Expect Forgiveness Can Do

Expectations for Myself
Example: There will be no fighting at the Thanksgiving dinner table.

Expectations for Others
Example: If we don't fight at the table, maybe Dad won't drink so much.

The Purple Blob

Issues involving forgiveness are often like a purple blob swirling around our heads. We can't seem to sort out whose problems are whose. We sometimes blame others for things we have done to ourselves. We sometimes blame ourselves for things that were done to us by others. We may confuse sadness with self-pity, anger with sadness, and excitement with anxiety.

The process of forgiveness involves sorting out our feelings, thoughts, attitudes, realities, and expectations.

When we can see clearly what our expectations are, we can begin to see where we are headed, and we can determine if we want to go there. Otherwise, we may just stumble along through our lives, trying to avoid as much pain as possible, trying not to hurt anybody. We deserve to live with more awareness than that.

Now that you have your list of expectations, on the following page put them into one of two categories: realistic and unrealistic.

This is not intended to be a way for you to judge and condemn yourself for expecting too much or too little of yourself or others. This is simply an assessment of your expectations.

Some of your expectations may seem to belong in both categories. If so, then put them in both. Sometimes we simply don't know if we are being realistic or unrealistic and *that is okay*. Confusion is forgivable.

These lists will not help you become a "good little boy" (or girl). They will, perhaps, help you to become more realistic about what forgiveness can and cannot do for you at this moment.

Begin to list your expectations in the categories "realistic" and "unrealistic."

My List of Expectations for Myself

Realistic: **Unrealistic:**

_____   _____

_____   _____

_____   _____

_____   _____

_____   _____

_____   _____

_____   _____

_____   _____

_____   _____

_____   _____

_____   _____

_____   _____

_____   _____

_____   _____

_____   _____

_____   _____

My List of Expectations for Others

Realistic: **Unrealistic:**

What Do You Really Expect?

What feelings came up as you began to assess your expectations in terms of what is realistic and what is unrealistic?

_____

_____

_____

_____

_____

Did you begin to feel sad as you realized that, realistically speaking, you might not get all the results you want, at least right away?

_____

_____

_____

_____

_____

Did you realize that you deserve to get more out of your relationships than you are getting?

_____

_____

_____

_____

_____

There are no right or wrong answers to these lists.

Everyone is unrealistic at times. If you expect that you won't need downhill skis for your Florida vacation, that is realistic. If you expect that it will not rain in Florida during your vacation because rain wouldn't be fair to you, that is unrealistic.

How realistic are your expectations about your work on forgiveness? Can you see how discomfort, frustration, and blame are the inevitable result of unrealistic expectations?

Later in this workbook, we will work on eliminating unrealistic expectations from the blueprints of our relationships. But, for the moment, these are just tiny steps aimed at sorting out our feelings about issues of forgiveness. Try to look at them calmly, without harsh judgment. Just the fact that you are reading this workbook is an indication that you have earned the right to expect to experience healing.

We will never, throughout this workbook process, discard the possibility of grace. Grace is a quantum leap in healing that is not directly attributable to what you have or have not done. At any point in this process you may experience release from anger, pain, or blame in a way that none of us could have predicted. Do not discount the possibility of miracles.

But you also should not discount the necessity of hard work.

BEFORE WE CAN FORGIVE

BEFORE WE CAN FORGIVE. . .

Before we eat, we want to know what we are eating. Before we sign on the bottom line, we want to know what we are signing. Before we forgive, we need to take a closer look at what we are forgiving. This is the "doing our homework" part of forgiveness.

The only way around is through. There is no way to investigate the choice and process of forgiveness without first getting in touch with the uncomfortable feelings that caused you to refuse to forgive, or that made you incapable of forgiving in the first place.

Forgiveness is not amnesia. It is not a drug we take to forget the pain. Forgiveness is not a bitter pill we swallow in hopes it will cure our relationships. Forgiveness is not a convenient escape route from the pain, anger, and sadness trapped within us—or the work required to understand and release those feelings.

If you have difficulty with forgiveness, you are not alone. Few doubt that forgiveness is basically good. Then why, as I questioned earlier, is there so little evidence of it? Where is the evidence that we live in a forgiving world? Why, in my local bookstore, did I find forty books on anger and three on forgiveness?

Forgiveness is not an act so much as a way of life. Forgiveness is a constant and spontaneous process of letting go.

Some people think you're crazy to want to try to forgive those who hurt you. Why would you want to choose to forgive when getting even may be more fun and immediately effective?

Let's admit it. There are lots of good reasons not to forgive. Can you think of any? On the following page, write a list of reasons why you would choose not to forgive, why you feel incapable of forgiving, or why you are confused about whether it is a good idea to forgive.

Reasons Not to Forgive

Examples:

> *I am afraid that if I forgive him, he will turn around and abuse me again.*
>
> *Forgiveness is a cop-out.*
>
> *I want her to go to her grave knowing I won't forgive her.*

Your reasons:

_____

_____

_____

_____

_____

_____

_____

_____

_____

_____

_____

_____

_____

A Word about Reasons Not to Forgive

There is a lot of pressure placed on us to forgive. Some comes from people who don't know how to do it any better than we do. Many of these are uninformed, not only about how to forgive, but about why or why not to forgive.

We have the right to question. Anything—like forgiveness—that is so much talked about and so little practiced deserves to be discussed openly.

I encourage you to trust your thoughts, feelings, insights, and intuitions. I am on your side. I believe you if you say you have good reasons why you can't or won't forgive. Forgiveness is a choice. Only you can decide if and when to embark upon the process of forgiving.

No matter what your stance may be on forgiveness issues in your life, awareness will always be the first step of change. Just as it benefits you to know exactly what you are trying to forgive before you can experience any success with it, you may want to know why you can't or won't forgive, so that you can be more at peace with your decision.

Here is my list of some personal reasons why someone might choose not to forgive. Did some of these appear on your list? If you can identify with some of the following items, feel free to turn back to page 43 and add them to your list.

If some items appear on your list that do not appear on mine, feel free to write me in care of this publisher and I will consider updating the list for the next printing.

A Partial List of Reasons Not to Forgive

- I have the right not to forgive.

- I am not ready to forgive.

- Forgiveness seems like too much work.

- Withholding forgiveness is a good way to punish the person I'm mad at.

- Forgiveness gets in the way of my denial of what my relationship is really like. In order to forgive, I have to admit to the problems.

- I am afraid of letting those old resentments come up again.

- I am afraid you might continue to hurt me, whether I forgive you or not. So why bother?

- I seem to need the highly charged emotional drama that forgiveness might interfere with.

- While I'm struggling to forgive others, they might see how vulnerable I am, and then they can find new ways to hurt me when my guard is down.

- By not forgiving, I can continue to feel superiority over and contempt for the person who abused me. I like being righteous and "one up."

- When I think about forgiving, I feel like a quitter and a loser. I feel as if I've been defeated in my attempt to prove the other person wrong. Forgiveness is a wimpy thing to think about, let alone do.

- When I forgive someone, I feel that I am, in a way, condoning the behavior. In a way, I am saying that what that person did to me was okay.

- Forgiving feels as though I'm letting the person off the hook, and I don't want to do that. I want that person to hang there awhile and suffer.

- Not forgiving is my way of setting limits about what is acceptable and what is not acceptable.

- I equate forgiving with forgetting, and I will never forget what was done to me.

- I will not forgive someone who will not accept responsibility for the wrongdoing by admitting it to me.

- I will not forgive because the person I am trying to forgive doesn't want to be forgiven.

- I will not forgive because my family is united by anger, not forgiveness, and I don't want my family to feel that I am getting healthier and leaving them behind.

- I will not forgive because we might have to start talking to each other, and I have mixed feelings about that. Silence is painful, but golden.

- Forgiveness messes with my favorite alibis, such as "I would have been a success if I had come from a healthy home where I received the love and nurturing I needed to achieve success."

- If I don't forgive my parents, then I won't be called on to provide primary emotional or financial care for them when they become old or ill.

- I won't forgive because that will destroy my definition of myself as a victim. I will have to begin to look at the ways I victimize myself by not assuming responsibility for my own life, despite who harmed me and what I have been through.

- I am reluctant to forgive because that feels like finally leaving home and I am not sure I want to disengage that much from my family.

- I don't want to forgive because I am afraid of moving on to whatever lies beyond the anger and blame.

Not everyone will be willing to admit to the above items. A lot of them may not seem "nice." But an open, honest inventory of your own resistance to forgiving will help you, whether you decide to forgive or not.

Take time to read over your list and mine. Give yourself credit for your honesty. The process you are now engaged in takes a lot of courage. Please refrain from clubbing yourself over the head for the items on your list. We are not human beings trying to be perfect. We are perfect beings trying to be human.

OBSTACLES TO FORGIVENESS

Obstacles to Forgiveness

On tours and in workshops related to my work on forgiveness, I discovered that there are indeed a few people who are just plain mean and nasty, who don't want to forgive because forgiveness gets in the way of their nastiness. There are also some who feel they are morally superior to the ones who harmed them. They base their lives on being unlike those who hurt them. Still others don't want to grow up and accept responsibility for their own lives, so they specialize in blaming others for their own difficulties.

But, by far, most of the people I have talked to are stuck in an unforgiving stance because of one or more of these reasons:

1. They don't know how to forgive.

2. They have come to believe that forgiveness is unnecessary or impossible.

3. They are often discreetly encouraged not to forgive.

Some obstacles to forgiveness begin within us. They are personal and individual and reflect our unique life situations. Others come from outside—from the society we live in or from our cultural or religious heritage.

There are many societal and doctrinal influences that affect our attitudes about forgiveness.

When well-meaning people say to you, "Let bygones be bygones" or "Why don't you just let go?" these comments may be interpreted as, "Don't think about how that person used you, and don't allow the deep feelings of hurt to surface."

Did you grow up with a vengeance mentality, "an eye for an eye, a tooth for a tooth"?

Were you exposed to a militant religion that is intolerant and unforgiving of all others?

Conversely, did you hear anything in church or synagogue that made you feel pressured to forgive? Does that pressure sometimes make you feel like not forgiving, especially if you believe that others in that institution don't try to understand how you feel and how difficult forgiveness is for you?

Did you read a book or see a film that told you that you must forgive but didn't give you a clue as to how?

Begin your lists now of cultural, societal, or doctrinal slogans or statements about forgiveness. How do they help or interfere with your attempts to forgive?

Cultural or Societal Obstacles to Forgiveness

Please answer these questions:

When it comes to forgiving, is it easier for men or women to forgive?

_____

_____

_____

_____

_____

_____

_____

Are either men or women expected to be better able or more willing to forgive?

_____

_____

_____

_____

_____

_____

_____

Do you believe either men or women do most of the forgiving?

_____

_____

_____

_____

_____

_____

_____

_____

_____

What longstanding societal grudges or attitudes create obstacles to forgiving?

Examples: Ethnic rivalries, or cultural encouragement to follow a rule of "Don't get mad, get even."

_____

_____

_____

_____

_____

_____

_____

_____

Religious or Doctrinal Obstacles to Forgiveness

Did you learn anything as a child, in church or synagogue, that told you there was one particular way to view forgiveness?

Example: "Father, forgive them, for they know not what they do."

_____

_____

_____

_____

_____

"Pray for them" is a wonderful, loving suggestion. Can prayer alone work for you in forgiving another person?

_____

_____

_____

_____

How does lack of evidence of forgiveness between and within religions influence your thinking?

_____

_____

_____

_____

Some Doctrinal Contradictions or Obstacles to Forgiveness

If you found it difficult to list nonpersonal obstacles to forgiveness, you're not alone. Sometimes there are obstacles working against us that we can't even see.

The work we are doing now is a process through which we begin to distinguish and separate our obstacles to forgiving, so that we can see them more clearly.

Let us look at a few obstacles to forgiveness that you might have picked up at your church, synagogue, or other place of worship. Even if you were not brought up in a religious family, you probably have been influenced by the religious values of a society founded on Judeo-Christian principles.

For example, I was never baptized and I never visited a church at any time during my childhood, yet whenever someone mentions an apple in a garden, or a fig leaf, or a serpent, the Garden of Eden registers in my mind. Few are isolated in their own culture.

Many churches in the Judeo-Christian tradition ask us to forgive, even though God does not always seem to be particularly forgiving. If God is all-wise and forgiving, then why did Jesus have to plead with God from the cross to forgive the people who were crucifying him? One assumption is that God was ready to pounce on the sinners until Jesus interceded on their behalf.

Forgiveness is sometimes presented as a mandated Christian principle by some theologians who do not seem particularly capable of or committed to forgiveness. That apparent contradiction, coupled with the fact that forgiveness is mandated in the first place, can be a huge obstacle to persuading people to forgive. People often rebel against what they are told to do, especially when double messages are involved. For instance, a missionary church orders a tribe of native peoples "to forgive those who trespass against us" as it trespasses on the tribe's "pagan" religion.

Forgiveness is often presented by the church as an "act" that has an immediate and specific "result." You "do" forgiveness. But when people attempt to forgive persons who have wronged them, and a while later discover that those persons wrong them again, they feel that either forgiveness doesn't work or that somehow they don't know how to "do" it "right."

A church cannot help but function, on some level, as a supreme parental authority figure. Even the most liberal church (or "parent") is subject to receiving potshots while parishioners (or "children") are developing spiritual awareness, coming to terms with who they are and where they came from, and sorting out their own beliefs.

In my experience, the transference of feelings about a family structure onto a church is particularly strong in people who were subjected to domestic violence or abuse. They often believe that forgiveness is difficult enough without feeling that the church is trying to shove it down their throats.

It would be helpful if forgiveness were presented as a choice. People are troubled enough if they are struggling with issues of forgiveness, without feeling pressure to "do" forgiveness "right." Presenting forgiveness as a choice takes the pressure off people who are already burdened.

It would also be helpful if our religious institutions were to view forgiveness as a process. As we rethink and rework our relationships with the people (or institutions) we are striving to forgive, we often find ourselves forgiving people we have already forgiven. As I began to forgive a painful incident that happened between my father and me, a memory of another event often would surface to take its place and demand to be looked at. It takes time to become fully aware of what and whom you are trying to forgive. It takes even more time to become ready and willing to forgive.

Forgiveness is more a journey than a destination.

Forgiveness is more a way of life than a fact of life.

Biblical questions can present obstacles to forgiveness. Christ said, "Father, forgive them, for they know not what they do." Christ didn't say, "Please take a few moments to toss around the possibility of forgiving them, Lord, for they are not the most together people I've ever seen." The mandate is to forgive.

Many people have difficulty understanding the need to "forgive them for they know not what they do." Why should we, and how can we, forgive all those who have harmed us but were ignorant of their motives? My brother, for example, did not intend to be the favorite son. But he was. And I have difficulty forgiving him for that, even though I know it was not his fault. Whether he knew what he was doing, whether he intentionally tried to be the favorite son or not, does not negate my feelings. Being aware that he was not in control of the situation—walking a mile in his moccasins—leads me to understanding, and understanding helps, but understanding is not the same as forgiveness.

Another often-quoted scripture that can create an obstacle to forgiveness is "Judge not that ye be not judged." The very process of forgiveness implies a judgment. You are in a position to offer forgiveness because, in your "judgment," you have been wronged. The other was wrong. You were right, and you were hurt. Seeing yourself as a victim and someone else as the victimizer is a necessary judgment in the process of righting a wrong.

Wouldn't it be better to tell people that they have the right to judge the behavior and attitudes of others? Judging behavior and attitudes is not the same as judging on the basis of their inherent worth as human beings. For example, people have to be able to judge when someone has gone too far and crossed a physical or emotional boundary.

The same is true of self-judgment. I need to be able to accept that "I made a mistake," without believing that "I am a mistake." When we talk about forgiving, the presence of painful feelings is implicit. If these feelings are not encouraged to surface in an atmosphere of safety, then little progress will be made. People are often tempted to call themselves names like "stupid," "bad," "self-pitying," or "ungrateful" when painful or embarrassing feelings come up. This only makes a painful situation worse.

Institutions should encourage people to accept that there is no such thing as a "good" or a "bad" feeling. There are only comfortable or uncomfortable feelings. Some feelings, of course, are valued more highly than others. Love, for example, is valued more highly than hate. But does that make hate "bad"? Is jealousy "bad"? Not if it gets you out of a relationship that does not merit your trust. In this case, jealousy, if not "good," would at least be "appropriate." Placing moral labels on feelings triggers guilt and shame, which stunts the growth of forgiveness. If people judge themselves too harshly, forgiveness becomes impossible.

Clichés like "Forgive and forget," "Let bygones be bygones," and "To err is human, to forgive divine" reinforce the acceptance of certain "nice" feelings. These clichés allow people to sweep difficult issues under the carpet in the name of forgiveness. "To err is human, to forgive divine" is a great invitation to divide a world of struggling people all over again into sinners and saints. It is also a great invitation to feel lowly and out of God's grace if you are having difficulty forgiving.

In my workshops, I encourage people to rewrite any clichés and quotations that make them feel "wrong" or "bad."

Another obstacle to forgiveness (judging by how often I am confronted with it at my lectures and workshops) is the commandment to "honor thy father and thy mother." I respond by saying that I do not consider it an act of honor to sweep my feelings about my family under the carpet in order to preserve the illusion of peace. I believe, instead, that finally getting my true feelings out in the open, so we can talk about them, is an act of courage, love, and honor. If I did not love and honor the people who have harmed me, I would be more inclined to ignore my feelings and to bypass the difficult process of forgiveness. *I honor my parents and others with my truth.*

In order to give and receive forgiveness, we must learn that forgiveness is not a religious or moral issue. It is a personal issue that can have religious implications.

There is no religiously correct or universally agreed upon approach to forgiveness. Our actions, more than our words, indicate that we aren't as forgiving as we claim to be, or even want to be, let alone being as forgiving as we think we "should" be.

Some tell us to be careful about forgiving because it might be equated with forgetting, which can lead to a repeat of the offense. Others tell us there is nothing to forgive, because all of life is in God's plan. Still others tell us we absolutely must forgive, but they can't tell us how. We have come to the conclusion that there is no conclusion. However I shall venture one.

Forgiveness is helpful, but optional.

I feel a whole lot better as a result of having successfully forgiven my parents and other people in my life. But I would probably still be in pretty good shape if I had decided not to bother with forgiveness at all. I was a pretty good guy before I forgave my parents, and I am a pretty good guy now. My relationship with God was good before forgiveness, and it is still good.

My work on forgiveness began to soar when I realized that all my previous attempts at forgiveness were focused on pleasing God or winning back the love of the person I was trying to forgive. I learned that the proper focus of forgiveness is the person doing the forgiving (me), more so than the person being forgiven.

Forgiveness is freedom from bondage to the past.

When we are encouraged to view forgiveness as a route to freedom for ourselves, more so than freedom for others, then it makes more sense for us to forgive. Then we don't feel that forgiving is letting the others off the hook so they can abuse us again. Forgiveness is an appropriately selfish thing to do.

- When we are encouraged to view forgiveness as a choice that only we can make, then we feel like we are being treated as mature, reasonable, trustworthy human beings.

- When we are encouraged to view forgiveness as a process, we are free to grow in spiritual ways at our own pace.

- When we are encouraged to allow all our feelings to surface, even the uncomfortable or embarrassing ones, then we are able to enlist our entire being in the process of healing.

- When we are encouraged to view forgiveness as an honorable thing to do, then we are free of the shame that would otherwise limit us.

- When we are encouraged to believe that we are not being judged unfairly, then we feel free not to be so hard on ourselves.

- When we are encouraged to see that forgiveness is not a "right or wrong" issue, then we are free to approach it in spiritual ways.

Personal Obstacles to Forgiveness

Now that we have written and talked about some obstacles to forgiveness that come from outside of us, let's consider some personal obstacles to forgiveness, the kinds that come from within us.

On the following page, list your feelings or attitudes that might interfere with your experiencing true forgiveness.

Once again, remember not to judge your feelings. Let your deeper feelings and attitudes flow from your heart onto the paper, where you can see them clearly.

Write your list of personal obstacles to forgiveness now.

My Personal Obstacles to Forgiveness

Please answer these questions:

How do I feel about my unwillingness or inability to forgive? Do I accept it? Am I proud of it? Do I think less of myself for it?

_____

_____

_____

_____

_____

Do I believe that most healthy people find it easy to forgive?

_____

_____

_____

_____

_____

What in my character or personality explains my difficulty with forgiveness?

_____

_____

_____

_____

_____

Do I feel I am expected to teach myself how to forgive? Is that possible for me?

_____

_____

_____

_____

_____

_____

Other personal obstacles to forgiveness:

_____

_____

_____

_____

_____

_____

_____

_____

_____

_____

_____

_____

_____

Some Thoughts about Personal Obstacles to Forgiveness

I would be presumptuous to write about *your* personal attitudes toward forgiveness, because my list would only be a reflection of *my* personal attitudes toward forgiveness.

I have, however, detected a few similarities in the lists honed from my workshops.

One major obstacle people tell me about is that the very thought of forgiving someone brings them face to face with lost hope. When we approach the option of forgiveness, we may have to give up hope for the chance of finally making the family right. Many of us still cling to our paintbrushes, years after the canvas has dried, waiting for the opportunity to change the picture.

Forgiveness often begins with a sigh. Defeated in our attempts to manipulate and control people, events, and outcomes, we often approach forgiveness as a last resort. We often arrive at forgiveness with the realization that the war is over and we did not win. That's the bad news.

The good news is that, like alcoholics who are asked to give up an old life in order to become eligible for a new one, we have arrived at the threshold of a new beginning.

But words like "new" and "beginning" and "change" are often scary for us. Holding onto resentments may—at first—seem safer, even if more uncomfortable.

Another personal obstacle to forgiveness is the withholding of our forgiveness until the other person accepts responsibility for what he or she has done to us. Some may not be able or willing to assume responsibility for their actions. Some we are trying to forgive don't care at all whether we forgive them or not. Does that mean, then, that we have to suffer from painful resentments for the rest of our lives? Only if we are not willing or able to overcome our own obstacles to forgiveness.

Another obstacle is that we often use resentment as a means to keep us separated from our true feelings. If we stare long enough at other people's failings, then we won't have to look at our own.

It is not that we aren't willing to forgive, but we claim that the other person doesn't deserve to be forgiven. But do *we* deserve freedom from resentment and pain?

What other personal obstacles make us unable to forgive?

_____

_____

_____

_____

_____

_____

_____

How about anger and blame?

_____

_____

_____

_____

_____

_____

_____

FACE TO FACE WITH ANGER

An Introduction to Anger

One day I was coming out of a conference with a friend whom I consider my primary spiritual advisor. I had just given a presentation and was feeling extremely fond of myself. We went into a nearby restaurant and, as I was looking at the menu, I told him my bike had been stolen from the door of the conference, where I had parked it.

"Your bike was just stolen and you're looking at the menu, getting ready to eat? Where are your feelings? Where is your anger?"

I explained that I didn't want to get angry now, because if there was any time when you should be able to handle adversity, it was right after you had given a convincing speech on spirituality.

"If Jesus Christ himself had walked out of that meeting and found that his bike was stolen he would have been furious!" my friend said emphatically.

I thought about it. I remembered Jesus in the temple, trashing the tables of the moneylenders. Yeah. He was right. Jesus in the Bible is quite often angry. What did happen to my anger? Why wasn't I furious that my bike had been stolen?

The world is full of differing views on anger. Jehovah of the Old Testament and Allah of Islam are both angry, vengeful gods. The God of my childhood was a white male who was always enraged and looking for someone to take his feelings out on. But Taoism and Buddhism emphasize the eradication of anger, overcoming it. Whose God was right? What is the best way to deal with anger? When is it justified and when is it pouting?

We have all experienced anger, and we all have opinions about it. We may see anger in ourselves one way and anger in others totally differently. In other words, we may encourage ourselves to get the anger out, while feeling terrified when other people do the same.

Is the quality of anger different because of gender? Are men more angry than women? Why are women encouraged to get sad, but not angry? Why are men encouraged to get angry, but not sad? Why are women told to speak softly and remain polite at all times? Why are men told they don't get angry, they get even? Both sexes suffer from stereotyping. And we all suffer from our lack of information about healthy anger.

Not all cultures divide emotions into slick compartments. Some cultures have one word to define both anger and sadness, whereas we might claim they are totally different emotions. Who is right?

Anger is universal. The expression of anger is cultural. Attitudes about anger—and the rules we have learned that govern our attitudes and behavior—can put us in conflict with other cultures. Ever noticed? Some cultures produce people who seem wildly emotional in public. They believe in venting, in letting it all out. Other cultures advocate emotional restraint to the point where a public display of anger would bring shame upon the family. Still other cultures think a public display of anger is not so much shameful as it is childish.

In addition to cultural differences, there are also personal differences. Some people like to rant and rave when they get angry. Some people get quiet when they get angry.

Anger is difficult to understand because rarely is it a specific, single emotion that is causing us pain and trouble. Emotions are complicated and they combine in different ways. Do you become afraid when you get angry? Then why don't you always get angry when you become afraid? Is anger the cause of your problem, or the result?

I am sure that most of you were not encouraged to have all of your feelings in your childhood homes. My father, for example, had a monopoly on anger. He was the only one in my family who was allowed to express it. And his anger was almost always followed by violence. It was not safe for me to express my anger openly, so I went inside with it, where it fermented and gained power over me.

Let's look at the role of anger in our families and in ourselves.

The Roots of Anger

Our angry responses to life seem to be provoked by three basic things:

1. Life situations.

2. Other people and their behaviors.

3. Our attitudes and beliefs.

Many people are angry about what happened to them when they were children. Wouldn't it have been nice to have been told by parents and teachers that it is okay to feel love, anger, resentment, hatred, fear, joy, jealousy, and many other feelings?

My daughter has all these emotions, sometimes all at once. Nobody calls her crazy or inappropriate. Sometimes she is laughing while she's crying. Sometimes she's crying while she's laughing. Her emotions whip across her face like summer storms on a Caribbean island. As soon as you can identify one emotion, she has moved on to another. That's healthy childhood.

A lot of us never were able to express emotions in a healthy way. Instead of getting love, we got angry. Many of us, as adults, pleaded with life, "Don't take away my anger, its the only thing I know."

Kids are angry. Adults are angry. Employees are angry with employers, and employers are angry with employees. The mood on the streets is often angry.

Just what is there to be angry about? Why is there so much anger around?

For many of us, there are a few undeniable truths that really make us angry.

Here are a few of them:

- We are angry because we can't be what we want to be when we grow up.
- We are angry because we think we deserve it all and we only get a portion of it.
- We are angry because life is not fair.
- We are angry because we can't successfully control or manipulate other people, places, or things.
- We are angry because we have to die.

My Personal Experience with Anger

Answer the following questions:

Was the expression of anger taboo in my family?

I don't think so — my father acted angry alot.

Was anger the only emotion I was allowed to express?

no

What are some of the things that make me angry? Things don't make me angry – Peop

When I am lied to
when someone breaks a commitment do
to me.

When I am abused or treated
without respect –

When my choice & dignity are
taken from me.

What about myself makes me angry?

When I can't control my
craving for sweets or over eating
When I am late
my hair
my body
my aging face & Body (skin)

What about other people and their behavior makes me angry?

Being taken advantage of:
  1. lies
  2. manipulated
  3. abused

Complete this sentence with as many examples as possible:

"I get angry when other people. . ."

lie to me

cheat on me

betray a trust

What triggers my *fear* of anger?

Social workers aren't supposed
to vent anger — or appear
angry. I must always appear
calm and in control or I will
be thought of as undependable.

Complete the following sentence with as many situations as possible:

"When I imagine expressing my anger, I fear. . ."

people will not trust me
people will think I'm out
of control

What I Can Do Instead of Getting Angry

Even people who are pretty good (or maybe too good) at expressing anger find times when they don't dare express their anger.

Make a list here of things you do instead of getting angry.

EAT food
EAt chocolate
get sad
cry
loose energy & withdraw

A Partial List of Things People Do Instead of Getting Angry

The following list of things that people often do instead of getting angry is not intended to alienate anyone who has engaged in any of these behaviors. My intention is simply to illustrate that, despite how scary or unpopular the expression of anger is, it may be better than at least some of these substitutes.

- getting violent
- having an affair
- engaging in brutal gossip
- denying that anger exists
- rationalizing our refusal to accept anger
- offering unsolicited advice to provoke others into anger instead of getting angry ourselves
- stuffing other feelings in an attempt to avoid anger
- transcending anger through meditation or prayer
- exercising vigorously *Tried-helped*
- indulging in raging monologues
- *talking about* anger rather than *feeling* anger
- *acting* angry instead of *being* angry
- blaming others instead of being angry at ourselves
- resorting to passive-aggressive behavior, such as subtle put-downs or chronic lateness.

You can see how anger can be a huge obstacle to forgiveness.

The point here is not to talk you out of your anger, but to provide you with choices.

At some point you may find that your problem is no longer *getting* angry, but *staying* angry.

Remember:

The goal of healthy anger is healing.

Obstacles to Owning and Expressing Anger

Just as we have seen that there are some very understandable obstacles to forgiveness, there are also a lot of obstacles to owning and expressing anger. We have already mentioned that fears can block people from getting in touch with their anger.

Am I afraid I will discover just how deeply sad and hurt I am underneath the anger?

yes — I have never completely delt with the sad & hurt that has come my way

Am I afraid I will hurt someone in my anger?

no

Am I afraid that someone will hurt *me* if I unleash my anger?

no

Am I afraid of being known as volatile or unreasonable?

yes

Additional Obstacles to Expressing Anger Appropriately

ALCOHOL AND OTHER DRUGS

I trust that you have worked hard on your personal lists and now have a much clearer sense of anger in general, the role of anger in your family, your personal experience with anger, things that trigger your anger, and things about anger that frighten you. Good work.

I want to add a few important insights into anger, in case they never made it to your lists.

Drugs and alcohol are tremendous impediments to getting in touch with and learning to express your anger appropriately. You do not need to be a recovering alcoholic or drug addict to have issues with forgiveness. But you do need to be in a clean, clear, sober state of mind and body in order to receive the gifts that forgiveness brings. What you do with your life once you are through with this workbook is none of my business. But, while we are involved with this process, I strongly suggest you give yourself the gift of sobriety.

Learning the art of forgiveness requires that you be in a physical and mental state receptive to not only the work but the grace that accompanies it. Don't stumble numbly through the miracle.

THE REAL DANGER

When I was in early recovery from substance abuse I asked an elder to tell me about anger.

"Put a 'D' in front of it" he told me. Putting a "D" in front of my anger spelled "Danger." That scared me, so I stopped working on my anger for a long time, until I realized that stuffing my anger was more dangerous than expressing it.

LOSING CONTROL

Another obstacle is the sense of losing control. Many of us prefer to control our feelings, not realizing that control can result in a buildup of emotions that begin to control us. Learning that we don't always need to be in control of our emotions means that we can begin to be more spontaneous with them. This workbook can help you realize that you need not be a slave to nor a dictator over your emotions.

ISOLATION

Another obstacle to the expression of anger is isolation. If we don't let people near us when we're angry, then they can't see it.

OTHERS' REACTIONS

If they can't see our anger, then we don't have to be embarrassed or ashamed of having it.

VULNERABILITY

We might not want to express our anger because we don't want to feel vulnerable. People will know how much we care if they see how emotional we can become. Then they might manipulate us.

PERFECTIONISM

Expressing anger messes with our perfectionism. Some have a high investment in having other people see them in a certain way. They want to appear perfect. Appearing red-faced, with eyes flashing and veins bulging on your neck because you are furious, doesn't do much for your good looks or your reputation of being cool under fire.

Other Things to Remember about Anger

My work in this area began with a refusal to be trapped by my own anger. I began to let go of willfulness and to work on willingness to let go of my angry stance. I began to focus on my willingness *to do whatever it took* to let go of anger.

Once you do some initial work on anger, you may begin to accept the possibility that you might wish to confront directly the person who's the object of your anger—when you feel sure that you can do so by focusing on yourself and without unnecessarily escalating the conflict.

Once we acquire some experience with expressing anger appropriately, we can loosen our rigidity. Often our anger is provoked by our refusal to be flexible.

We can learn to respect time and timing. People are quick to blame themselves and others for not moving quickly when *someone else* decides it is time for us to make a change. We make inroads in this area when we ourselves are ready—and not a moment sooner.

Our anger can be reduced if we let go of our unrealistic expectations. We can begin to allow others to be imperfect.

We can be willing to do the grief work called for with the demise of any relationship, even poisonous ones.

We can learn that the opposite of anger is not love; it is indifference.

We can learn that anger draws attention to a problem but doesn't do much to change it.

BLAMING OURSELVES, BLAMING OTHERS

SELF-BLAME

Many of us express our anger by turning it inward, into self-blame. Sometimes we feel justified in this behavior. We feel that the reality, the truth of the matter, is that we *are* to blame, and should therefore, rightfully, be punished.

List here some situations or behaviors you blame yourself for.

I blame myself for

_____

(what I've done to myself).

Example: I blame myself for being forty pounds overweight.

I blame myself for

_____

(what I've done to my family).

Example: I blame myself for not being a successful provider for my family.

I blame myself for damaging my relationship with

_____

Example: My boss. I blame myself for getting fired.

BLAMING OTHERS

Many of us express our anger by turning it toward others. Sometimes we feel justified. We feel that the reality—the truth of the matter—is that they are to blame, and should therefore, rightfully, be punished.

List here some attitudes or behaviors that affected you and for which you feel others are to blame.

I blame

_____

(for what happened to me).

Example: I blame my boss for firing me.

I blame my family for

_____

(what happened to me).

Example: I blame my family for my being forty pounds overweight.

I blame

(for affecting my relationship).

Example: I blame a sexist boss for my unsuccessful work relationships.

A FURTHER LOOK AT SELF-BLAME AND BLAME

Self-Blame

If you could purchase insurance for self-blame it would be called "my fault" insurance. No-fault insurance would be inconceivable to a self-blaming person.

Often self-blame is a manifestation of the internalization of childhood traumas we endured. We may blame ourselves for being ill, for example. We may believe illness is a punishment for having done something wrong or bad. If a cold strikes the day before a major speech or performance, we blame ourselves for not having been more in touch with our bodies.

Sometimes we blame ourselves for getting angry. Or we blame ourselves for not being as good as the people working next to us.

Anger and blame directed against ourselves is self-victimization. It is self-punishment, which can be related to abusing ourselves with excesses, which can lead to addiction. Sometimes we punish ourselves because we blame ourselves for what went wrong in our relationships.

A way out of self-blame is to learn and accept that not *everything* in life relates specifically to us personally. Blame and self-blame are often attempts to explain to ourselves the reason that something bad happened. That's the logic at work when we blame ourselves for getting sick ("I got sick because. . .").

But sometimes things happen simply because they happen, and they aren't about us and what we did or didn't do. We simply aren't that powerful. This perpetual need to have an explanation— a source of the discomfort, a cause and effect—is a reflection of our need to control. We fear chaos, randomness, wildness, and meaninglessness. Blaming ourselves and others gives us a temporary sense of safety.

The explanation doesn't save us from the anger and pain of what went wrong, but at least we know the cause of our suffering, or so we think. The cause is me. The cause is you. The cause is anybody we can lay blame to. We crave a sense of fairness in the world. Clearly, it doesn't always exist.

When people get furious and shout, "Why did this happen to me?" and I reply mildly, "Why shouldn't it happen to you?" they think I am cold. I think I am accepting of the mystery of life. Sometimes bad things happen to good people. Sometimes good things happen to bad people. Very young children die in car crashes. Nazi criminals lead long lives of luxury in South America.

We look for meaning in places where it just might not be. We can't accept a bumper sticker that says, "Shit happens." We want it to say "Shit happens for the following reasons:. . ." We want to know what we did to deserve certain outcomes. We want to comprehend the incomprehensible by assuming full responsibility for the inexplicable. We use "if only" and "I should have" statements. We believe some or all of the following:

- We made it happen.
- We didn't do what we could to stop it.
- We didn't do what we should have done to start it.
- We expect too much or too little of ourselves.
- We aren't enough.

What is the payoff for self-blame? The payoff is a sense of control. If I am powerful enough to have caused the problem in our relationship, then I just might be powerful enough to stop it.

Self-blaming people, in an attempt to get out from under the weight of their own judgments, sometimes try to strike deals with God ("I will dedicate my life to you, if only you will promise that I will never have to go through *that* again.") Then probably we will realize God doesn't need to bargain.

The issues of control in a self-blaming person are further illustrated by reasoning like this: "If I am to blame for what happened, then I can learn to control what happens by pinpointing the feelings and attitudes that caused it to happen. I will control the feelings that cause me trouble. When I can control my feelings and attitudes, then I will have also begun to control your reaction to me. Then you won't be able to hurt me anymore. All I have to do is to replay over and over and over again in my head just what went wrong. When I see exactly what *I did to cause it*, then I will get rid of that part of me and we will never come close to breaking up again."

This illustrates the convoluted thinking that accompanies self-blame. When you blame yourself, you have found a reason for everything "bad" that happens. Then you can try to control your own and others' behavior so that it won't ever happen again.

Blaming others

What is the usual dynamic when self-blame shifts to blaming others? Who are the most logical people to blame? Of course! Parents!

Mother-blaming or father-blaming is often a major obstacle to developing and building selves separate from those of our parents. Parent-blaming stands in the way of addressing problems in a constructive, creative way. When we run out of parent-blaming, we can then shift the blame again. We can blame God, fate, genes, lovers. Blaming persons and powers outside ourselves for our troubles makes us perpetual victims. And victims who were raised by victims and grow up to marry victims produce victims, unless they become willing to change.

> **Blame is an attempt to avoid taking responsibility**
> **for your part in the problem, as well as your**
> **part in the solution.**

Each person claims that the only way to break a stalemate is for the other person to become more responsible. This can result in couples never really being able to come together, and never really being able to come apart. How many people do you know (yourself included?) who are still, years after the initial problem began, hugely angry at a former lover or spouse?

Isn't that horrible? Perhaps not! Perhaps they hold on to the blame and anger because it was—and perhaps still is—the only thing that made them feel close. Anger and blame can feel very intimate. Holding on to blame and anger, people never really have to let go. Unfortunately, they may become divorced from the persons but remain eternally married to the problems.

Many find it hard to assume responsibility because the very word *responsibility* often implies assuming the *blame* for what went wrong. They feel accused and become defensive. So they avoid responsibility.

Blame is an attempt to get others to feel responsible for our feelings. We say things like, "You made me feel this way" and "If it weren't for you. . . " When we stop blaming each other, we can start to be concerned for each other and be more responsible to—and for—ourselves.

ANGER, BLAME AND FORGIVENESS

SOME CONCLUSIONS ABOUT ANGER, BLAME, AND FORGIVENESS

A nger is a misrepresented emotion. Many assume that anger is bad because it results so often in pain and injury. But anger can be positive when it warns us that our boundaries are being violated. Actually, expressing anger in healthy ways can prevent violence by notifying others to stand back, stop pushing, and leave us alone.

At this point in your process of exploring forgiveness, you have gotten in touch with some of the issues in your life that provoke anger and blame. Many of you have never experienced or expressed anger because it didn't feel safe to do so. If that is your situation, then you might want to sit with your anger for a while, to claim it as your own, to practice expressing it appropriately, to explore where it came from, to see how it helps and how it hurts you.

If your anger is primarily against yourself, you may find that you desperately seek someone to blame for causing you so much anger and pain. If you have done the work in this workbook, you may realize that much of the "blame game" is futile and irresponsible. But it is also important to realize that knowledge and insight frequently do not translate directly into changed behavior. In other words, if blame comes up, go ahead and blame. If you feel anger, then get angry! These are your feelings, and you are entitled to them.

The real work with forgiveness begins after we feel we have run the gamut on anger and blame. Sometimes we find we have learned to *get* angry, but we don't yet know how to avoid *staying* angry. *If this is not where you are yet, then stay exactly where you are now.* Remember again that forgiveness takes time and timing. We live in an instant coffee, instant breakfast, instant replay society that tries to rush us along, perhaps before we are ready to move.

Have you ever sat in a restaurant where you just received your entreé when some waitperson or manager tries to hurry you because there are people waiting for your table? Pretty annoying? Don't hurry yourself here. You are entitled to sit at this table and digest this information for as long as you like.

Just because you suspect you aren't ready to realize the effects of this work on forgiveness does not mean that you cannot benefit from working through this book to the best of your ability. I have discovered, through my workshops throughout the country, that, more often than not, people are much healthier than they think they are.

If you are not quite ready for this work, then you may not now experience great relief. This does not mean that you are rigid or stupid, or that this workbook is ineffective. You are ready when you are ready. You may find it useful to read my book, written three years earlier, entitled *Forgiving Our Parents* (CompCare Publishers). It is an exploration of forgiveness that may help prepare you for the work being done here.

While some are not ready to forgive, many are ready and don't know it. You cannot lose by reading about and working on this material.

At this moment, I strongly suggest that you stop reading this and bless yourself for being a good person who is trying hard to become a better person. What more can you ask of yourself? Say this, out loud if possible:

"Bless you, _____(your name), for being a good person who is trying hard to become a better person."

Now let's roll up our sleeves and do some hard work on letting go of blame and anger, a prerequisite of our work on forgiveness.

LETTING GO OF BLAME
AND ANGER

Now, let's roll up our sleeves and do some hard work on letting go of blame and anger, a prerequisite for our work on forgiveness. Remember. . .

1. Take what you like and leave the rest.

2. Don't berate yourself for what you cannot yet translate to your own situation.

Here are some tools for letting go of some of the blame and anger that may have surfaced during your work with this book. Also included here are some insights on the Twelve Steps, for those who are familiar with them. Selected Steps are adapted here to pertain specifically to anger and blame. The original Twelve Steps of Alcoholics Anonymous are reprinted on page 139.

Letting Go of Anger and Blame

■ Learn to accept your feelings.

■ Learn when to express them appropriately.

■ Take responsibility for your intentions and motives in expressing anger.

■ Be willing to accept responsibility for ending the conflict, even if you are "right."

■ Avoid anger as a control device. Screaming at people so they will give in or back down is not appropriate conflict resolution.

■ Define what you will and won't accept from others.

■ Keep the focus on yourself. (Self-focus is not the same as self-blame.)

■ Stick with "I" statements. Avoid "you" statements, such as: "You made me do that."

■ Respond—don't react—to perceived accusations.

■ Learn to listen.

■ Deal directly with the source of conflict. Avoid third parties. Talk—don't gossip.

■ Be prepared for shifts in relationship dynamics. If you have always been angry with someone, you may find it hard to accept kindness from that person.

■ Don't blame yourself for what was done to you.

■ Don't blame others for what you did to yourself.

■ Don't focus on what you should have done. That is living in the past.

■ Identify with other people—don't compare. (Lots of us are angry because we think we didn't get as good a deal as someone else.)

■ Learn to be flexible. Be willing to change.

■ Identify sources of misinformation (stereotypes, lies, rumors).

■ Let go of the need to be right.

- Grieve. (We use anger to avoid the pain of this necessary process.)

- Be polite. Be civil. Respect the spark of divinity in each of us.

- Seek healing of your perceptions. (Often our perceived slights against us are imagined or exaggerated.)

- Learn to forgive yourself.

Some Twelve Step Applications

1. Admit we are powerless to control our feelings.

2. Accept that a power greater than ourselves can restore us to balance.

3. Turn our anger and blaming over to our Higher Power.

4. Take a written inventory of feelings, causes, and patterns of our behavior.

8. Make amends for what we did. But also give up our shame and allow others to be responsible for what we didn't do.

10. Make a periodic check for anger and blame. Learn to face them promptly.

11. Tap into the power of prayer. Pray for deliverance from anger and blame. Pray for the well-being of those you are angry at. (It works!)

*See page 139 for the original Twelve Steps of Alcoholics Anonymous. Numbers here refer to the corresponding original Steps.

FORGIVING OTHERS

CONSIDERING THE CHOICE OF FORGIVING OTHERS

Now that we have experienced some ways of letting go of blame and anger, perhaps we can begin to experience forgiveness.

On the following page, write in the blank spaces at the top of the page the name of the person, group, or institution—whomever and whatever—you are considering forgiving. The person you are considering forgiving could be your parent, lover, boss, or anyone you feel has wronged you.

Write a list of attitudes, actions, behaviors, you are attempting to forgive. Be specific. Take some time doing this. Allow yourself to be as angry, vindictive, sad, lonely, indifferent, cynical, relieved, or loving as you feel. Mention specific incidents, as well as all your feelings and thoughts associated with them.

Remember that you have a choice as to whether to forgive or not. Writing about issues, incidents, and feelings doesn't commit you to forgiving. You don't owe someone forgiveness simply because you are considering it. But you do owe yourself honesty. You may not be comfortable with some of the feelings that come up. But they are your feelings. Bless your feelings by accepting them for what they are, not for what you wish they were.

Try not to judge your feelings harshly. (If you start calling yourself names, your Higher Self or inner child might withhold information from you, so as to avoid being yelled at again.)

Coax your deeper feelings out of you by declaring that this is a safe place to experience your feelings without shame or judgment. This means loving and accepting yourself the way you are.

Remind yourself that you need not show this list to anyone.

Considering the Choice of Forgiving

I am willing to consider forgiving the following. . .

ACTIONS
Example: Being fired by my boss.

_____

_____

_____

_____

_____

_____

BEHAVIORS
Example: My lover always completes my sentences for me.

_____

_____

_____

_____

_____

_____

ATTITUDES

Example: My grandmother believes women are the weaker sex.

_____

_____

_____

_____

_____

_____

These are my thoughts and feelings connected to those actions, behaviors, or attitudes:

Examples:

- ■ Rage
- ■ A lust for revenge
- ■ A sense of injustice
- ■ Humiliation
- ■ Fear of not finding another job

_____

_____

_____

_____

_____

_____

_____

_____

_____

WRITING A LETTER THAT WILL NEVER BE MAILED

You have now begun to discover some of the underlying issues of blame, anger, and forgiveness that you have with others and yourself. By now, you may have listed throughout this workbook a series of brief descriptions of your feelings.

You now have an opportunity to communicate your thoughts, insights, and feelings in a letter to the person (or persons) you are struggling to forgive. Write the letter to your parent, lover, boss or whomever.

Do not worry about spelling, punctuation, beautiful language, perfect margins, or any constructions that might divert you from your purpose. *Your purpose is to get the feelings out and gain some perspective on your relationship problem(s).* You might even discover some things that you like about the relationship.

Ask the "editor" who is sitting on your shoulder and judging your letter as you write it, to kindly keep his or her mouth shut. You are not creating literature. You are writing an important letter. If you have great difficulty writing, try it anyway. No one is looking. This letter will never be mailed.

If you still can't seem to write, consider investing in a little, inexpensive, hand-held tape recorder. When my mother died suddenly, I was too emotionally devastated to write. My hands were shaking. I was crying. And I was in a lot of pain that I was not very anxious to embrace. I was also traveling a lot at the time. I used the hand-held tape recorder to get my thoughts and feelings out. When I could, I went home and transcribed the tape. Then I read it back to myself.

A lot of it was garbled, nonsensical, overtly sentimental, sickeningly self-sympathetic, and downright awful. So what? I didn't care that I was a writer by trade who was supposed to be good. I just wanted some relief and some perspective on what I was going through. And that is exactly what I got—first from talking into the tape recorder, again from transcribing it onto paper, and then again from reading it back to myself. I was three times blessed with insight and perspective.

I still occasionally use that tape recorder. When I am troubled, I sometimes take the tape recorder to bed with me and put it under my pillow. If I wake in the middle of the night, I can record my dreams and feelings without even turning on the light. Then I transcribe them onto paper in the morning. Often I have no idea of what is bothering me until I use the tape recorder or paper and pen to get it from inside of me to outside of me, where I can see it in black and white. This process works.

If you have trouble writing and have a tape recorder, here is an alternative plan. Place two chairs in the middle of a room facing each other, a few feet apart. Sit in one chair. Hold the tape recorder in your hand and face the empty chair. Imagine the person you are struggling to forgive in the chair across from you and begin to speak to that person. Pour it all out, honestly—all your love, hate, fear, sadness, fond memories. Take as long as you like, but don't stop too soon. If you can't think of what to say, just stare at your "manifestation" of that person until the words come.

When you've finished talking, thank the person for listening, say good-bye, and transcribe the tape recording onto page 97, the page reserved for your letter to the person you are struggling to forgive.

Keep your letter simple. You need not aim for eloquence, dramatic shifts in the relationships, psychological breakthroughs, buckets of tears, gobs of forgiveness, or anything other than the true expression of your thoughts, insights, and feelings. This does not necessarily have to be fun. It also does not necessarily have to be torture. It is what you make of it. The only rules are those you impose upon yourself.

On the next page begin to write your letter to the person you are struggling to forgive.

My Letter to _____

Dear _____,

_____

_____

_____

_____

_____

_____

_____

_____

_____

_____

_____

_____

_____

_____

_____

_____

_____

_____

_____

_____

_____

_____

_____

_____

RECEIVING A LETTER THAT WAS NEVER MAILED

Now write a response to the letter you just wrote to the person you are struggling to forgive.

Imagine that you mailed your letter you just wrote. Imagine seeing that person open your letter and read it. Study the facial expression as the person reads your letter, puts it aside, picks up a pen and paper (or sits down at the typewriter or computer) and writes a response to your letter.

On the following page, write a response to your own letter. Do not try to be like the sender. Simply allow his or her words to flow from your pen. Let that person have a say. Don't think, analyze, or react to the words as you are writing. Just let the letter happen.

I have written the first line of the letter. Go on from there.

_____*'s Letter to Me*

Dear _____(your name):

Thanks for your letter.

_____

_____

_____

_____

_____

_____

_____

_____

_____

_____

_____

_____

_____

_____

_____

_____

_____

_____

_____

_____

FORGIVING
OURSELVES

CONSIDERING THE CHOICE OF FORGIVING OURSELVES

Our issues of forgiveness seldom involve *only* others. To one degree or another, we all have difficulty forgiving ourselves for blunders made or opportunities missed.

If we are unforgiving of our parents, then, on some level, we must surely be unforgiving of others. If we are unforgiving of others, then, on some level, we must surely be unforgiving of ourselves.

What might we consider forgiving ourselves for?

For example, many of us believe we were responsible for the troubles in our family. We might believe that, if we had been better children, our parents would have been better parents.

What issue of forgiveness do you have with yourself? Was it something you did that you just can't seem to forgive yourself for? Was it something you didn't do? Did you fail to live up to someone's expectations of you? Did you fail to live up to your own expectations of yourself?

On the following page, write a list of the things you are struggling to forgive yourself for. Remember, this section is about any issue you have with *yourself,* not others.

Don't worry if some of the same items on this list also appear on your list of what you are struggling to forgive others for. If something you discover in this section gives you insight into issues you have with others, turn back the page and add it to the previous section, "Considering the Choice of Forgiving Others."

When you make this list, stick with "I" statements ("I feel that I am a failure because I. . ." instead of "you" statements ("You made me feel that I am a failure because you. . .").

Once again, be gentle with yourself. Don't judge your feelings harshly.

Now begin your list of things you are considering forgiving yourself for.

_____

_____

_____

_____

_____

_____

_____

_____

_____

_____

_____

_____

_____

_____

_____

_____

_____

Things I Am Considering Forgiving Myself for

I am willing to consider forgiving myself for the following. . .

ACTIONS

_____

_____

_____

_____

BEHAVIORS

_____

_____

_____

_____

_____

ATTITUDES

_____

_____

_____

_____

_____

These are my thoughts and feelings connected to those actions, behaviors, or attitudes.

_____

_____

_____

_____

_____

_____

_____

_____

To Forgive Others Is to Forgive Ourselves

For the sake of illustration, let's assume that your letter was written to your parents. Of course, not everyone's primary issues of forgiveness are with parents. Perhaps your main issues are with your spouse or sibling. But not everyone has a spouse or sibling, whereas everyone has parents. Whether you like your parents or not, whether you have ever met your parents or not, we all have parents and we all have issues with them.

Perhaps you feel your parents deprived you of the ability to sustain an intimate, romantic relationship because they abused your ability to trust. Perhaps you wrote a sentence like this, "If it weren't for you, I would have been a success," because you feel they never held you in high regard and you, therefore, never held yourself in high enough regard to do what was necessary to become successful. Perhaps you think they caused your illness or depression.

From your letter to yourself that you wrote as coming from your parents, what did you learn? Did you discover that the lines are often blurred between what we are striving to forgive ourselves for and what we are struggling to forgive others for? Did you discover how you may be struggling to forgive them for what *you* did to yourself? Or did you discover how you have been blaming yourself for what they did to you? Did you see yourself blaming your parents for blaming you, or criticizing your parents for criticizing you?

Did you discover that you are not particularly forgiving?

Did you find yourself repulsed by their plea for your forgiveness?

Did you discover you are very angry with yourself for allowing them to direct your life?

Did you find that you have a terrible time letting forgiveness in because you don't know exactly what to do with feelings of love for people you've always thought you hated?

Did you discover that, no matter how severe their abuse of you was, they could never have done to you what you have done to yourself?

Take the letter you wrote to your parents or others and look for phrases, words, or sentences that illustrate what you believe they did to you. Look for sentences like the one above ("If it weren't for you, I would have been a success"). Highlight or underline those words or sentences.

Now substitute the word "I" or "me" in the place of "you," or "him," "her," or "them." Substitute "I" for a specific name such as "Mom" or "Mary" or "Dad" or "Bob." Using this technique, the sentence would now read,

"If it weren't for *me*, I would have been a success."

Does that sound true? It may or may not be. I don't know your specific issues of abuse, or how ready you are for the forgiveness process. If it doesn't sound true, that's fine. But quite often people find the words "I" and "you" interchangeable in their two letters.

For myself, writing these two letters helped. I knew that my parents were very troubled people. What they did and didn't do to and for me caused me great difficulty in getting on with my adult life. But they weren't smart enough—or cruel enough—to trip me up every step of the way to success and happiness. Not the way I tripped myself up! I took their knack for abuse, used it on myself, and made an art out of it.

I do not hate myself for having done that. I do, however, find it very sad. And I do find this insight extremely beneficial to my spiritual growth. I stared at my parents until my eyes hurt, and then I reluctantly began to look at myself. I discovered that my parents live in my head, where they are still thirty-four years old and addicted to booze and cruelty. In actuality, my mother is dead and my father is an old, broken man who almost never leaves his house.

It is my perceptions of my parents that I need to change, not my parents themselves. Strapping others with the responsibility for what I have done to myself causes me to remain a perpetual adolescent. My assumption of responsibility for the choices I make, the attitudes I keep, the love I risk is what brings me a glimpse of freedom.

A Few Thoughts on Forgiving Ourselves

Have you ever sat in your room, staring out the window, feeling a little down, watching people walk by? Don't they look great? They are bopping along, looking clean and fresh, having kissed their loving families good-bye so they could hurry off to their meaningful jobs, which are fascinating parts of their meaningful lives.

We might imagine these lucky people with no holes in their socks, no blemishes under their makeup, no ghosts in their closets. They appear well rested from their weekends at the beach with flawless lovers, who have high-visibility, lucrative careers in environmentally safe, politically correct, charitable organizations.

And what about us? If we break a shoelace, we can trace it back to having been raised in a troubled family. We are flawed human beings who consider ourselves miserable failures at being perfect rather than what we are: terrific successes at being human. We put ourselves at a spiritual and psychological disadvantage because we can't seem to forgive ourselves for not being the persons we think we should be.

We could all use a dose of self-forgiveness. Often all we really need is to forgive ourselves for being human. Quite often we don't know what we're doing, and that had better be okay if we wish to maintain a semblance of serenity. Our goal is to be able to accept ourselves, even for what we don't like about ourselves.

To forgive our own humanity means that we have to be able and willing to forgive others' humanity also. This same judge within us who wants to punish other people for making a mistake will eventually want to punish us for making the same or even a lesser mistake.

Serenity does not come from confessing the sins of others. Beyond recognizing what happened and how we feel about it, by continuing to focus on the harm others have done to us, we negate the responsibility we have to ourselves to undo the wreckage of the past. We can learn to accept ourselves for who we are rather than who we think we should be.

When we let go of our unforgiving stance, we let go of the grip we allow others to have on us. Unforgiveness perpetuates the suffering *in us* and does nothing to end it. What follow are a few attitudes and behaviors that we might consider forgiving ourselves for.

Forgiving Ourselves for. . .

Here are a few things we might consider forgiving ourselves for:

1. Not being able to cure or save our parents or other loved ones.

2. Not living up to our parents' expectations of us.

3. Making mistakes, not being a perfect child.

4. Not being able to save or cure our siblings or our own children.

5. Treating ourselves the way our parents or others treated us.

6. Abandoning ourselves when the going got tough (siding with our enemies, going into emotional shutdown).

7. Developing the same dysfunctions we deplored in our parents. We may have become exactly like the person(s) we hated.

8. Being judgmental.

9. Depriving ourselves of success.

10. Depriving ourselves of the ability and willingness to take risks.

11. Depriving ourselves of a relationship to self, others, and God.

12. Being our imperfect selves.

13. Being human. (Remember: Only saints and dead people never make mistakes.)

A Few Thoughts on NOT Forgiving

Earlier in this workbook we took a look at some very understandable reasons not to forgive. We talked about not being ready. We talked about a person's own right to determine what is forgivable and what is unforgivable. We talked about how forgiveness sometimes feels as if we're letting the person who harmed us off the hook too easily. All of these and more reasons mentioned earlier make a lot of sense.

Let me restate that there is no one, other than you, who has the right to judge you in a negative light because of your inability or unwillingness to forgive.

But the lack of forgiveness *may* signal that something more is going on besides our rightful and understandable refusal to forgive and forget what has been done to us. For example, we may use unforgiveness as a way of punishing our parents or other loved (or unloved) ones who have harmed us. Our conspicuous absence at social gatherings, our refusal to return phone calls, our chronic lateness, our inappropriate laughter or tears—these can all be indirect ways of paying people back for what they did to us.

The only practical choice in the process of forgiving others is to keep the focus on ourselves. To forgive our parents is to finally leave home. To forgive our boss or co-workers is finally to be free of the unhealthy dynamic in our workplace. To forgive a lover is to reclaim the power we gave up when we chose to let his or her approval of us be the bait that kept us biting at the hook.

Forgiveness of others began to make a lot of sense to me when I realized that not forgiving them was like punishing them by holding my breath. When I was a kid and I held my breath, it certainly alarmed those around me. But I was the one who turned blue and passed out.

What is the benefit of not forgiving? What reward is there for holding onto the blame and anger, rage, and resentment?

Many times the only thing left of our relationship with someone is the anger and righteous indignation we feel toward them. In my own life, I was still having blazing arguments with my former wife two years after our divorce. I couldn't seem to break the pattern, even though I saw that our daughter was being hurt by our refusal and inability to get along.

Through my work on forgiveness, I realized that our love was long gone. Our working toward a common goal was gone. Our dreams were dead. Our concern for each other's health, our interest in each other's interests—all cold. The only thing left with any heat was the anger. When I dropped the anger, I came face to face with my own sadness. It was only then that I was able to begin to grieve over the loss of a marriage that had ended two years earlier.

I finally realized that by holding onto pain and anger—refusing to let go of it—I had become the victim *and* the abuser in my life. I was a victim because I had been abused. And I was an abuser because I insisted on remaining a victim.

By not forgiving, we hurt ourselves as much, if not more, than we hurt the person who harmed us. By not forgiving, we often are the ones who are pumped full of anger and adrenaline, while the persons who harmed us are having nice, untroubled naps on couches somewhere.

Learning this did not make me feel I had to forgive. It simply helped me realize that I was the ultimate beneficiary of the process of forgiveness. I didn't want to be someone who didn't dare get into another relationship because of being unable to let go of the inevitable sources of anger that would arise. I began to see that. . .

**Nonforgiveness is an acid that eats away
at the shiny surface of love.**

FORGIVENESS: TOOLS AND MISTAKES

TOOLS OF FORGIVENESS

We have discussed—and worked on—forgiveness of others and forgiveness of ourselves. Now here are some actual tools of forgiveness that you may utilize at any time, whenever you feel the need for forgiveness.

Of course, not all of the tools on this list will apply directly to your life today. Certain tools will have relevance to your life at certain times.

At the end of the list are brief elaborations of points that deserve emphasis.

Tools of Forgiveness

1. Begin by letting go of our unforgiving stance.

2. Admit that the events and feelings really happened.

3. Admit that the past cannot be undone. There is no hope for a better yesterday.

4. Recognize that we need no longer be dependent upon parents or others for approval. Thus we take back our rightful power and learn to validate ourselves or seek validation from more sympathetic parties.

5. Release expectations that others will respond to our work on forgiveness.

6. Release unrealistic expectation of ourselves.

7. Accept others for who they are, rather than who we want them to be.

8. Set flexible rules of conduct for ourselves and others. For example, it is okay to say "You may not call me after 10 P.M. because I sometimes get too wound up and can't sleep."

9. Talk about issues as they come up, and encourage our children to do the same. That way, we might avoid having years of moldy, pent-up emotions to sort through.

10. Write a letter to our parents or other loved ones, telling them our feelings about what happened. We need not mail the letter.

11. Find a neutral party (therapist, sponsor, mentor, friend, member of the clergy) to talk to.

12. Learn not to take everything personally.

13. Learn to accept basic tenets of powerlessness.

14. Meditate, focusing on our need to forgive and to be forgiven.

15. Turn the other cheek.

16. Use your Higher Self in creative visualizations.

An Elaboration on Some Tools of Forgiveness

A discussion of items 5 and 6 of "Tools of Forgiveness" appeared in an earlier section titled "Expectations." You may wish to reread it at this time.

A tool for eliminating unrealistic expectations from your work on forgiveness is to make them "disappear."

Remember that it is our perceptions of our relationships that we seek to heal, not the relationships themselves. We have the right to choose to release from our minds any unrealistic expectations of others (or ourselves), and we don't need others' permission or their presence to do so.

Here is how to do it:

Close your eyes and become aware of your feelings. Think of a specific action you wish to forgive. Feel the anger the thought produces. State your feelings by completing the following sentence:

"I resent you because. . ."

Are you willing to let go of the anger? Are you willing to do what it takes to let go of the anger? Answer yes or no, out loud, if possible.

Now state what you wish could happen in order to make things better. Complete the following sentence:

"It would be better if you. . ."

Now make that unrealistic expectation disappear by completing the following sentence:

"I hereby release my unrealistic expectation that you. . ."

You now have a clean slate with that person where there used to be an unrealistic expectation.

Now we will replace the space where the unrealistic expectation used to be with something more realistic and positive. Read the following list three times, preferably out loud.

- I accept you as you are.

- I accept me as I am.

- I accept that you need not lead your life the way I think you should.

- I accept that you are not perfect.

- I accept that you may not desire forgiveness the way I do.

- I accept that you need not act in any particular way in order for me to have my feelings of love and forgiveness.

- My feelings of love and forgiveness exist in me, not necessarily between you and me.

- I accept that I am powerless over your essential self.

- I accept that I am powerful over my own attitudes and perceptions.

And then again:

- I accept you the way you are.

- I accept me the way I am.

Example: If someone lied to you, here is how the process would work.

"I resent you because you lie to me."

"It would be better if you always told the truth.

I hereby release my unrealistic expectation that you never lie to me and always tell the truth.

Now read the above list that begins, "I accept you as you are."

Notice that this process frees you from the tyranny of expecting too much from others. The process changes you. It does not necessarily change the other person. You still have a liar on your hands. You might ultimately choose to forgive, and then to disengage from that person because you don't want to be involved with a chronic liar. But at least you now have the awareness and tools to grant you a greater perspective of the relationship. You now realize it was very unrealistic, for whatever reason(s), to expect that person to be able to tell you the truth consistently.

Item 15 in the "Tools of Forgiveness" instructs us to "turn the other cheek." Does that notion make you feel sick? It has that effect on many. But we are free to experience, interpret, and perceive that adage anyway we wish. Here is how I feel about it.

All of us are part human and part divine. These two parts of our essential selves are often engaged in combat for dominance. For example, during the war in the Persian Gulf, many of us might have thought about the lousy parenting Sadaam Hussein might have received. On that basis—if forgiveness is indeed divine—we might have desired to forgive him for acting out his assigned role in his troubled family system. Another, very human part of us might have wanted to strangle the guy.

Just as in the situation of the two sisters struggling to decide whether to go home or not for their mother's birthday, both views are right and both views are wrong.

We can argue forever about the merits of forgiving others and ourselves.

For the sake of argument, let's refer to the abuse we suffered as a slap in the face. There is even a metaphor with broader interpretations of abuse: "Wow, was that ever a slap in the face!" One interpretation of turning the other cheek is to get slapped again, and that is what puts so many people off.

Let's now choose to interpret turning the other cheek to mean that we should turn from our human part to our divine part before we respond to the abuse. Let us imagine turning away from being hurt on our mortal, physical level and trying to respond from our divine component of self.

Why would we want to do that? If we are wounded in anger and respond with anger, what we will get in return is more anger. If we respond to hate with hate, we get more hate, and so on.

Forgiveness is a way of moving from one spiritual plane to another in order to receive divine assistance in dealing with what often seems like insurmountable problems. Sometimes I am so caught up in my own slough, it seems impossible that I will ever step on dry land again. I truly need to access my Higher Power and Higher Self in order to get to a place where forgiveness is possible. Knowledge is not enough.

Three Basic Mistakes Involving Forgiveness

Nobody's perfect. Considering there is so little written about forgiveness, it's a wonder we are learning how to choose to forgive in the first place. So it is not surprising that mistakes will be made along the way.

I made three basic mistakes when I first embarked on the process of forgiveness. I will elaborate on them, in the hope that you may avoid them.

Learn to recognize these mistakes:

1. It is a mistake to view ourselves as victims of the world we perceive. We are free to perceive the world and ourselves differently. We need not wait for others to change before we can experience forgiveness.

2. It is a mistake to withhold love in response to not having been loved. You cannot cure anger with anger, hate with hate, or the lack of love with the lack of love. You must be a model of forgiveness if you want to experience forgiveness. If you need to stay away from certain others because they are not good for you, forgiveness will help you do that. Through forgiveness, you will become detached from others' need for conflict, anger, or pain—thus ending the conflict between you and those others, as well as ending the conflict within yourself.

3. It is a mistake to underestimate the power of grace. Awareness, understanding, timing, tools, therapy, yoga, nutrition, exercise, friendship will all help clear an area where forgiveness can take place. But none of these will force forgiveness to happen. Forgiveness is a by-product of spiritual evolution. It is often visited upon us when we least expect it, or didn't know where to look for it. Forgiveness is "metaphysical" in the sense that it happens in the space between, or *along with* (meta) our "physical" world (the one that comprises what we do, think, eat, read) and the "spiritual" world. That is why prayer for the grace of forgiveness is highly recommended.

GOING HOME

Going Home

Whether or not we have problems with our parents, we all can benefit from some suggestions about going home. If you do not have this situation, perhaps you have a friend or co-worker who does and who can benefit from this information.

If you plan to go home to your family for the holidays, or for whatever reason, go to the home within yourself first, and then go home. Use techniques of self-forgiveness and self-love that you have learned in this book. Then you will be more centered and calm when you walk through the door to your family home, having first walked through the door to your own heart.

Release your family from your unrealistic expectations of what they will be like. Let them be themselves. You don't have to like the way they are in order to respect them. You don't have to love their behavior in order to love them.

Realize that you are no longer a child. You have choices. You have the choice to go or not. You can choose to stay in a hotel instead of in their home. You can choose if and when to confront your parents or others.

"Bookend" your visit home by calling a trusted friend before you go, and ask that same friend to be available for a call while you are there or after you come back, to talk about what is going on or what happened.

Be flexible whenever possible and, without expecting too much, remain open to the possibility of change for the better, even if it appears remote. Don't be defeatist and cynical. Try to respond, rather than to react, to what happens and what is said.

Have "Plan B" ready, just in case the situation becomes explosive and you have to leave abruptly.

Consider taking someone with you.

Schedule your time so as not to end up wandering around, disoriented, bored, or uncomfortable.

Allow yourself to say "no" and "can I get back to you on that?" when confronted by someone provocative who is demanding an immediate response.

Rehearse an exit speech that would not offend unnecessarily or hurt someone if you decide to leave early.

Check your motives and intentions. Do you secretly want a fight? Do you want to prove what jerks they are? Do you want to justify your own cruelty? Remember that honesty without compassion is cruelty.

Remember that, if you dread going home, you will probably have a dreadful time. If you are in awe of your family's negativity, then your time there will probably be awful. If you try to be polite and kind, you increase the chances of surprising yourself by having a pretty good time after all.

Agree to love and bless yourself no matter what happens. Take care of yourself. Remember that we, your friends, need you.

BEING ON YOUR OWN SIDE

BEING YOUR OWN ADVOCATE

When doing work on forgiveness, it helps to be on your own side. A lot of materials have been written about "getting in touch with your inner child." These writings assume that the inner child is a precious, loving, little person, who is all cuddly and willing to be rescued by us adults. That may be true.

My inner child was mute and didn't trust me a bit. Why should he? I was a self-abusive person my entire life. What was so different now?

I discovered that if I wanted to get in touch with my inner child and coax him back into the world, I would have to learn to love not only the precious, cute little boy within me. I would also have to learn to love the not-so-cute brat within. A child, even an inner child, knows when he or she is being loved conditionally.

My inner child helped me to learn that I am a wonderful person, as well as a pain in the butt sometimes. My life challenge is always to love and accept myself the way I am *at this exact moment.* It is easy to love myself when I am behaving well. But can I accept and love myself when I am being a jerk? Can I love myself twenty pounds overweight or underweight? Can I love myself when I am full of self-pity?

Chances are all of us have difficulty in always accepting ourselves. Self-acceptance is one of the goals of this workbook. But first we may have to accept the lack of a perfect relationship with ourselves.

Let us now take a tiny step in learning to love ourselves, even if we were never loved before. *Let us now be on our own side,* become our own advocate.

Pause a moment here and take a mental photograph that is about to pop into your head. Do not alter the image that is about to come to you. Just seize it, and see it. Now, see an image of . . . you as a child.

Close your eyes now for a moment and study the picture. Open your eyes when you are ready. Again, do not change the image that first popped into your mind. See yourself as a child.

After each of the suggestions that I am about to make, close your eyes, study the image, and open your eyes again when you are ready.

- Smile at the mental photograph you have of yourself as a child. Even if the image you have is of you in pain, smile at yourself. Even if you don't like the way you look, smile at yourself.
- Now walk toward the child that is you.
- Get down on your knees so that you are at eye level with the child.
- Smile into the eyes of the child that is you. Let your child see the love in your eyes. Let yourself see your smiling self reflected in the pupils of the eyes of your inner child.
- Now, in your mental image, stand up, take the child by the hand, and say to the child: "I am on your side. It is safe to be with me."
- Now, in your mental image, walk hand in hand with your child back to this moment, to this book.
- Close your eyes for one final time and review the images of self-love that you have just created.

Good work!

THE HIGHER SELF

There is a space, an atmosphere, that exists between our physical selves and our Higher Selves and God (or spirit, or whatever word you may choose if the word "God" offends you). Healing takes place in this space.

If you are violated by someone in an act of violence, anger, or hatred, you must go to your Higher Self in order to forgive. Instinct, intuition, and the healing spirit dwell in this atmosphere. Here you can find a free-flowing river of spirit force that can wash away the muck you are stuck in.

Remember that forgiveness is not possible on the same plane where the transgression took place. If you were hurt in anger or hatred, you cannot heal if you are still in anger or hatred. A problem forged in hate cannot be broken in hate. That is why we use visualization and meditation to bring us to higher ground.

So let's flex our spiritual muscles. Let's illustrate for ourselves how we can use releasing as a tool that is always there for us. Raise your consciousness by envisioning a loving relationship with your inner child and Higher Self. When you have done so, ask the forgiveness of your Higher Self for any specific thing you have done to another, or another has done to you. Feel the understanding, love, trust, and compassion that are there for your asking. Ask for the forgiveness of yourself or others. And then thank your Higher Self, or your Higher Power, whomever you choose, for forgiving you.

Tell yourself that you will continue to love and forgive yourself, even if you are unable to maintain constantly these feelings of forgiveness for yourself or others. Thank your Higher Power for being forgiving. Thank yourself for being able to receive forgiveness.

Say aloud to yourself, "Thank you, Higher Power and Higher Self, for being forgiving. Thank you for allowing me to be willing and able to be forgiven." Feel the goodness and the sense of freedom that are there waiting to be expressed.

Forgiveness Is. . .

. . .a boomerang

Some think that forgiveness is like an arrow. The forgiver shoots an arrow of forgiveness toward the person he or she is attempting to forgive. The arrow of forgiveness sticks right in the heart. The forgiver feels righteous. The forgiven repents. They live happily ever after.

But forgiveness is more like a boomerang than an arrow. It is launched by the forgiver, circles around the forgiven, and lands back in the hands of the forgiver. Forgiveness encompasses everyone and everything it touches.

. . .resurrection

Forgiveness is resurrection. It is not that resurrection *involves* forgiveness. Forgiveness *is* resurrection. Forgiveness is how we resurrect our relationships with the past, the present, and the future. Forgiveness is how we resurrect our relationships with each other. Forgiveness is how we resurrect our relationships with ourselves.

DEAR ME. . .

A LETTER TO MYSELF

Part of the process of forgiveness involves disengaging from others enough to accept that sometimes we have to stop waiting for someone to give us something that we might as well learn to give to ourselves. That is the purpose of this letter to yourself.

Write a loving letter to yourself. You may wish to acknowledge what you have been through, where you are now in your spiritual journey, and what hopes and dreams you have for the future.

Begin your letter on the next page.

I'm Going to Sit Right Down and Write Myself a Letter

Dear_____ (your name):

_____

_____

_____

_____

_____

_____

_____

_____

_____

_____

_____

_____

_____

_____

_____

_____

_____

_____

_____

_____

_____

Dear Reader,

That letter you just wrote to yourself was a wonderful way to end this book.

Blessings and health,

Dwight Lee Wolter

*To forgive our own humanity means
we have to be understanding
of others' humanity.
We forgive and accept others
so that we may be
forgiven and accepted by others.
Forgiveness of ourselves is an act
of love and compassion.
By acknowledging and forgiving
the limitations and excesses of others
we acknowledge and forgive
the limitations and excesses of
ourselves.
Thus forgiving others is
a wonderfully glorious and selfish
thing to do.*

Forgiveness is not an act, but a way of life.

The goal of forgiveness is not so much to forgive as it is to be perpetually, spontaneously forgiving, to clear a space where no resentment accumulates.

Forgiveness is like a river. You can never step into the same river twice because it is ever changing, ever flowing. At the place where you step into it, the water is always different.

Beyond forgiveness, there is no need to forgive. Beyond forgiveness, no judgment has been made. Beyond forgiveness lies pure, total, absolute acceptance.

About the Author

Dwight Lee Wolter is the author of three earlier CompCare books, *A Life Worth Waiting For, Forgiving Our Parents,* and *My Child, My Teacher, My Friend.* He is also the author of *Sex and Celibacy: Establishing Balance in Intimate Relationships through Temporary Sexual Abstinence* (Deaconess Press). Dwight Lee Wolter conducts seminars and workshops nationally on the subjects of forgiveness, blame and anger, parenting, and men's issues. He lives in Manhattan with his wife and child. For workshop information or to arrange for media appearances, call toll free 800/328-3331.

THE TWELVE STEPS OF ALCOHOLICS ANONYMOUS

1. We admitted we were powerless over alcohol—that our lives had become unmanageable.

2. Came to believe that a Power greater than ourselves could restore us to sanity.

3. Made a decision to turn our will and our lives over to the care of God, as we understood Him.

4. Made a searching and fearless moral inventory of ourselves.

5. Admitted to God, to ourselves, and to another human being the exact nature of our wrongs.

7. Humbly asked Him to remove our shortcomings.

8. Made a list of all persons we had harmed, and became willing to make amends to them all.

9. Made direct amends to such people wherever possible, except when to do so would injure them or others.

10. Continued to take personal inventory and when we were wrong, promptly admitted it.

11. Sought through prayer and meditation to improve our conscious contact with God, as we understood Him, praying only for knowledge of His will for us and the power to carry that out.

12. Having had a spiritual awakening as the result of these steps, we tried to carry this message to alcoholics, and to practice these principles in all our affairs.